D1449595

plant
life

To my husband Derek,
your support and encouragement
has made all of this possible.

To my fellow stitchers and friends,
may you enjoy stitching these
designs as much as I enjoyed
creating them for you.

paige tate
& CO.

- -

Copyright © 2019 Libby Moore
Published by Blue Star Press
Paige Tate & Co. is an imprint of Blue Star Press
PO Box 8835, Bend, OR 97708
contact@paigetate.com | www.paigetate.com

Photography and instructions by Libby Moore
Etsy® Shop: ThreadFolk
@threadfolk

ISBN 9781944515706

Printed in China

10 9 8 7 6 5 4 3

PAIGE TATE & CO.

Modern Makers Series

Thread Folk

a Modern Makers Book of Embroidery Projects
and Artist Collaborations

LIBBY MOORE

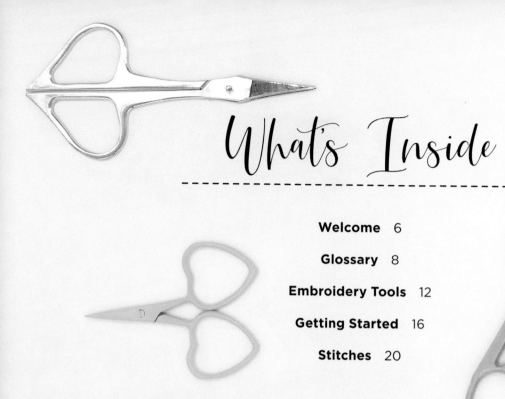

What's Inside

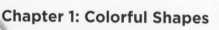

Welcome 6

Glossary 8

Embroidery Tools 12

Getting Started 16

Stitches 20

Chapter 1: Colorful Shapes 26

Project 1: Geometric Heart 28

Project 2: Confetti 34

Project 3: Abstract Hoop 38

Chapter 2: Florals 44

Project 4: Floral Curtain 46

Project 5: Leafy Wreath 50

Project 6: Gardener Girl 54

Project 7: Vase of Flowers 58

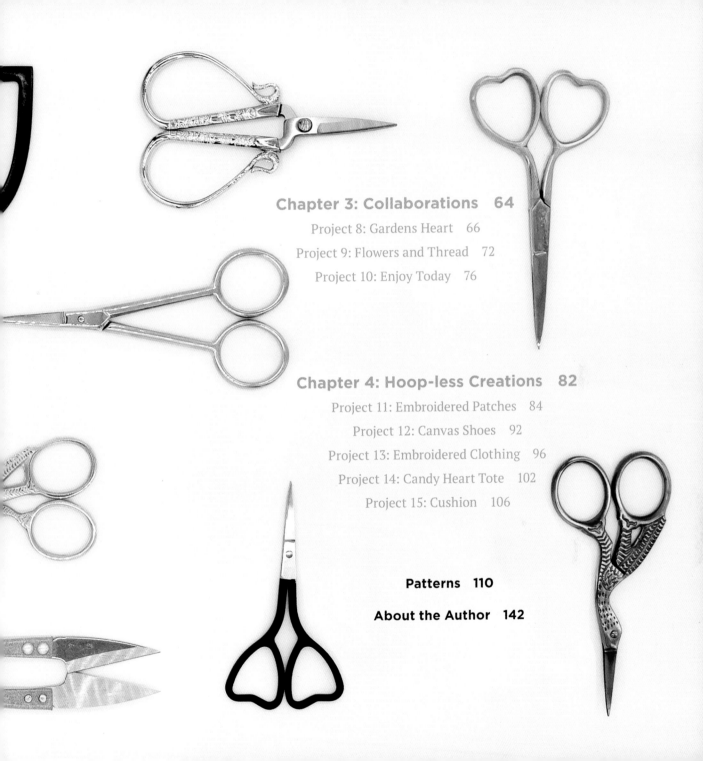

Chapter 3: Collaborations 64

Project 8: Gardens Heart   66

Project 9: Flowers and Thread   72

Project 10: Enjoy Today   76

Chapter 4: Hoop-less Creations 82

Project 11: Embroidered Patches   84

Project 12: Canvas Shoes   92

Project 13: Embroidered Clothing   96

Project 14: Candy Heart Tote   102

Project 15: Cushion   106

Patterns   110

About the Author   142

This story starts

with a Secret Santa gift exchange in 2013. The recipient was my sister-in-law and the gift was a personalized cross stitched family portrait of her, my brother, their girls, and their chickens (or chooks, to my fellow Australians!). It was a fun, modern take on the traditional family portrait. Aside from learning a little bit as a child, this was the first time I had cross stitched. With the help of online tutorials and an old embroidery book I picked up second hand, I taught myself and it was love at first stitch! The feeling of accomplishment that I received from teaching myself a new skill and creating something delicate and beautiful with it was wonderful. Naturally, I had to stitch my own family portrait next!

Using social media, I shared my creations with friends and family and the requests came rolling in to immortalize other cherished families in thread. As time went on, my work moved away from cross stitching families and evolved into creating embroidery patterns featuring a range of other fun embroidery stitches. I have been fortunate to collaborate with so many talented illustrators and painters to bring their designs to life with needle and thread. Together with these artists, I produced a range of modern embroidery patterns and kits, all intended to fuel the creativity of anyone out there who, like me years ago, wants to learn embroidery but doesn't know quite where to start. I wanted to help be a catalyst for others' creative journeys.

I love embroidery and the way in which this age-old craft has evolved time and time again to stay current and modern, all the while using the same embroidery stitches that have been used for generations. There's something special in that. I love that I can feel like I'm sitting in a Jane Austen novel, embroidering with the Bennett sisters, while I'm actually stitching an avocado patch to wear on my denim jacket!

I am absolutely ecstatic to bring this book of original embroidery projects to you, including a few very special designs that I have created in collaboration with some of my favorite artists. In this book, you will learn how just a few basic embroidery stitches can be utilized and manipulated to create beautiful, detailed, and delicate works of art. There really isn't anything difficult about embroidery. All it requires is patience and practice; you will master the collection of stitches featured in this book before you know it.

I hope that you will take the time to enjoy this slow craft, stealing some moments here and there to add a few therapeutic stitches to your fabric and to be proud of yourself as you see your creations unfold.

Happy Stitching!

Libby

Glossary

Back Stitch:
An embroidery stitch where stitches are sewn backward to the direction of the sewing.

Back Stitched Chain Stitch:
A variation of chain stitch where a row of back stitch is stitched over the top of a foundational row of chain stitch.

Calico:
Plain weave fabric usually found in white, cream, or unbleached cotton.

Carbon Paper:
A paper coated on one side with carbon or another pigmented substance. Used for transferring patterns to fabric.

Chain Stitch:
A series of embroidery stitches connected in a chain-like pattern.

Cotton Embroidery Floss:
Made of six individual mercerized strands, this is the most common type of embroidery thread.

Couching Stitch:
An embroidery stitch that uses two lengths of thread: a foundational length that follows the contour of the pattern lines and a fastening length that is stitched over the top of the foundation at various intervals, tacking it to the fabric.

Embroidery Hoop:
A tool to keep the fabric taut while stitching, which helps to keep stitches and tension consistent.

Fishbone Stitch:
An embroidery stitch where the stitches overlap slightly at a center point resulting in a braided effect, making it a great filler stitch for leaves.

Fusible Interfacing:
An additional layer applied to the backside of the fabric to add firmness and stabilize the work area. It is also useful to protect the backside of stitches on items that see frequent use (e.g. clothing). It has an adhesive side that permanently adheres to fabric when it is applied with an iron.

Fly Stitch:

A simple embroidery stitch that is shaped like a V or a Y, depending on the length of the tail. It can be worked horizontally or vertically, singularly or joined together in rows to create various effects.

French Knot:

An embroidery stitch that creates a small, tight knot.

Iron-on Adhesive:

Used for bonding fabric together without the need for sewing.

Lazy Daisy:

An embroidery stitch that is created with a single chain stitch, making it a great stitch for flower petals.

Long and Short Stitch:

A series of embroidery stitches that result in a brick-like pattern. A good stitch for filling larger areas and to use in projects where stitches are required to be short (e.g. embroidered patches).

Metallic Thread:
Made from polyester fibers, this thread adds a sparkling element to embroidery. It can be difficult to work with and is best used as a short single strand.

Perle Cotton:
Very high quality, non-divisible thread. It is highly mercerized, quite strong, and comes in a range of thicknesses.

Printable Water Soluble Paper:
A fabric stabilizer that can be put through a printer and adhered to fabric, making it an easy pattern transfer method. The paper dissolves in water, leaving only the embroidered fabric behind.

Satin Stitch:
An embroidery stitch consisting of rows of straight stitches placed close together. A good stitch for filling larger areas with thread.

Seed Stitch:
A series of small straight stitches placed in random directions to fill an area.

Straight Stitch:
The most basic of embroidery stitches, this long, straight stitch can be left on its own or stitched in groups to form shapes and patterns.

Whipped Back Stitch:
A variation of back stitch where a second strand of thread is woven through a foundational row of back stitch, giving a rope-like finish.

Water Soluble Marker:
Used to draw an embroidery pattern onto fabric. The marks are easily removed when rinsed under cold water.

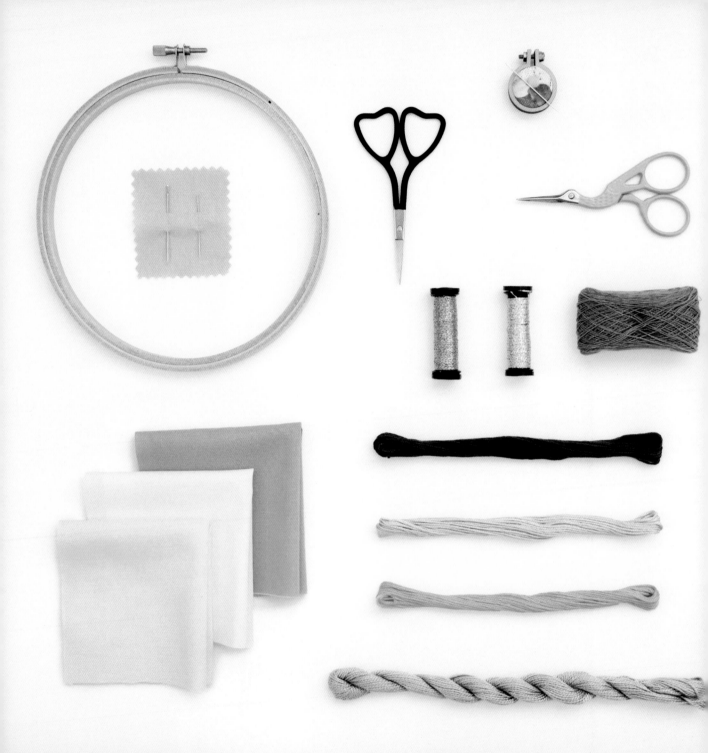

Embroidery Tools

Any artist would agree that having the right tools for your craft is very important. Thankfully, the tools required for embroidery are affordable and easy to come by. You can find everything you need in your local fabric store or online.

Thread

There are many different kinds and brands of embroidery threads available in varying thicknesses and finishes. Whichever kind of thread you choose to stitch with, it is important to ensure it is good quality. Cheap thread of poor quality can have a dull finish, be difficult to work with, and may not be colorfast. My preferred brand of thread is DMC®. This well-known brand produces high-quality, colorfast products.

Cotton Embroidery Floss: The most commonly used kind of thread is cotton embroidery floss. It is easy to source and comes in a wide range of beautiful colors. Cotton embroidery floss is made up of six individual mercerized strands. It is incredibly versatile as you can customize the thickness of the floss depending on how many strands you use.

Perle Cotton: Unlike embroidery floss, Perle cotton is non-divisible. It has a beautiful sheen and is incredibly soft to touch. It is highly mercerized, quite strong, and it comes in a range of thicknesses.

Metallic Thread: While pretty to look at, metallic threads are notoriously difficult to work with. If you choose to use it, it is best to stick with shorter lengths of thread and use only one or two strands at a time.

While the aforementioned threads are the most commonly used, I like to think there are no rules when it comes to creating modern embroidered art! This applies to threads as well as many other supplies. There are some beautiful specialty threads that can be sourced online or in boutique fabric or needlework stores. Silk thread, linen, woolen, naturally dyed, hand spun, and even metal threads are just some of the variations on traditional embroidery thread that one can find.

Fabric

When starting out with embroidery, look for quilting cotton or calico of good quality. Ideally, choose a fabric with minimal stretch in a light to medium weight. Linen is another popular choice for many embroiderers. However, you can stitch on almost any kind of fabric or material! You'll just need to make minor adjustments as you stitch, like paying attention to the tension of your stitches.

Hoops

Embroidery hoops come in a wide range of sizes and styles. They are intended to keep your fabric stretched and taut while you stitch. The most common—and my preferred style—are made from wood and have a metal screw at the top which is used to fasten the fabric between the inner and outer frames.

Needles

Embroidery needles come in a wide range of sizes. They have a larger eye than a regular sewing needle and a sharp point to easily pierce the fabric. The larger the needle number, the smaller the needle; they are usually found in a set that includes a range of sizes. I prefer to use a size 7 needle when I use three strands of thread and a size 5 needle when I use all six strands of thread.

Scissors

Embroidery scissors are small with thin, sharp blades that allow them to get as close to the fabric as possible. These days, embroidery scissors come in a wide variety of styles. While it's not necessary to have more than one pair, they can be so pretty to look at and fun to collect!

Fabric shears have long, sharp blades and are used to cut out the piece of fabric that you will embroider on.

Needle Minders

These clever little tools aren't necessarily a "must have" supply, however in my opinion, they are a game changer! Before I used a needle minder, I would search for my lost needle down the side of my couch cushion more times than I care to admit. A needle minder is fairly self explanatory. It is a little two-piece magnet to attach to your fabric to "mind" your needle between thread changes or when you put your embroidery away for a while. Like scissors, there are a lot of cute designs on the market.

Getting Started

How to hoop fabric:

1. Separate the rings of your embroidery hoop.
2. Lay the inside hoop on the table and center your fabric over the top.
3. Gently push the outer hoop down over the top and tighten the screw, pulling the fabric taut as you tighten.

Transferring Patterns

Tracing: Great for light-colored fabric, tracing doesn't require extra supplies. Tape your embroidery pattern to a window or place it on a light box. Place your fabric over the top, taking care to center the pattern. You may wish to tape the fabric to your window to help hold it in place. Use a water soluble marker (my preferred method) or a sharp lead pencil and trace over the lines of the embroidery pattern. Be aware that lead pencil marks will not wash out of fabric, so take care to trace lightly and with fine lines that you can stitch right over.

Carbon Paper: Great for darker fabrics. Simply lay the paper carbon side down on top of the fabric and then lay the embroidery pattern down on top of that. Use a ballpoint pen to trace over the lines of the embroidery pattern. If you use this method, keep in mind that carbon paper doesn't wash out easily, so be sure to cover all the transfer lines with stitches.

Water Soluble Paper: Trace the embroidery pattern onto water soluble paper and then stick it directly to your fabric. You can stitch right through the paper and fabric together. Once you have finished, soak your embroidery in cold water and watch the paper dissolve away! You may want to do a test on your fabric with this first, as it can leave a residue behind on some fabrics.

Separating Thread

Cotton embroidery floss consists of six individual mercerized strands of thread. Most of the time, you will only use two or three strands at a time. This means you need to separate the strands before you thread them onto your needle.

1. First, cut a length of thread (approx. 50cm/19in is a good length to work with).

2. Hold your cut length of thread in one hand between your thumb and finger. Lightly brush your finger over the ends of the thread to separate the strands from each other.

3. Gently separate the strands; pinch the desired number of strands between your fingers on one hand and the remaining, unneeded strands between your fingers on the other hand.

4. With the thread dangling, slowly pull apart the two groups of threads. You may need to pause and let them unwind a little around the halfway point as they may get twisted if you pull too quickly.

Starting and Finishing

When you're ready to start stitching, thread your required number of thread strands through the needle and leave a short tail. Knot the other end of the thread to secure it and stop it from pulling through when you're getting started. Experienced embroiderers may shake their head at this, as there are other methods to secure your thread. But for the beginners out there, lets keep it simple, shall we?

When you are finishing off a color or section of stitching, you can either knot off your thread or sew it through a few stitches on the back of your fabric to secure it.

Finishing Off the Hoop

If you use a water soluble marker (this is my preference), once you've finished stitching, simply give your fabric a rinse under cold water and gently dry by rolling up in a clean towel. Place another dry towel on your ironing board and lay your embroidered fabric face-down; gently iron the back. The towel underneath the fabric helps to cushion your stitches so that the iron doesn't flatten them.

To finish your embroidery in the hoop you will need:
- Your finished embroidery
- Embroidery hoop
- Ballpoint pen
- Fabric shears
- A piece of felt at least a bit larger than your hoop
- Embroidery thread that matches the color of your fabric
- Embroidery thread in a color of your choice
- Size 5 needle

To frame your embroidery:
- Separate the embroidery hoop.
- Lay the inner hoop on the felt and trace the outer contour of the hoop with a ballpoint pen.
- Cut out the circle of felt and set it aside.
- Refasten your embroidery into the embroidery hoop, pulling the fabric taut so that there is no puckering around the stitches.
- Lay the hoop on the table and trim the excess fabric approx. 1"-1.5" away from the hoop.
- Turn your hoop over.
- Using the embroidery thread that matches the fabric, thread your needle with enough thread to circle the whole hoop plus a bit extra for tying off at the end. Don't knot the end of the thread.
- Make a running stitch the entire way around the excess fabric. Be sure to leave enough of a tail of thread where you started the running stitch.
- Pull tight to gather the fabric and knot the threads in place to secure the gathers.
- Measure a piece of the embroidery thread in your chosen color that is at least three times the circumference of the embroidery hoop.
- Thread your needle with the long piece of embroidery thread and knot the end.
- Place the felt that you cut over the top of the gathered excess fabric.
- Starting from beneath the gathers, stitch a blanket stitch or another similar stitch the entire way around the felt circle, stitching the felt and gathered fabric together; finish off.

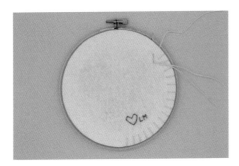 

Straight Stitch

- Bring the needle up through A and down through B.

Back Stitch

- Bring the needle up through A and down through B.
- Bring the needle up through C and down through A.
- Continue this pattern of bringing your needle up a space ahead and going back down into the same hole created from the last stitch you made.

Whipped Back Stitch

- Lay the foundation by completing the back stitch for the entire area you intend to "whip."
- Bring the needle up through A.
- Pass the needle under the A-B back stitch without piercing the fabric underneath.
- Repeat the previous step underneath the B-C backstitch, and so on, until you have whipped over the entire foundation layer.

Split Stitch

- Bring the needle up through A and down through B.
- Bring the needle up through C, passing through the middle of the A-B stitch, and down through D.

Satin Stitch

- Bring the needle up to the front of the fabric through A and down through B.
- Bring the needle up through C as close as possible to A, without going through the same hole created by A.
- Continue this pattern until you have filled in the area.
- When filling in an organic shape, you will need to overlap some of the stitches to follow the contour of the shape.

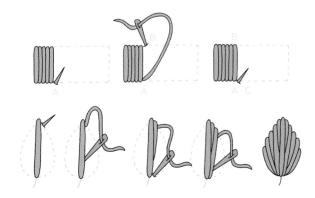

Fishbone Stitch

- Bring the needle up through A and down through B, making a short stitch along the middle line of the leaf.
- Bring the needle up through C and down through D.
- Bring the needle up through E and down through F, crossing the stitches over one another.
- Continue this pattern as you work down the leaf, creating a braided effect.

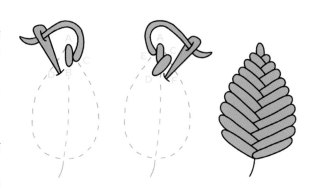

Chain Stitch

- Bring the needle up through A.
- Pull the needle down through A, stopping when you have a small loop left behind on the front side of the fabric.
- Bring the needle up through B, pulling the chain link behind it taut as you go.
- Repeat the previous two steps, pulling the needle back down through B and so on, catching each chain link with the next one as you continue the pattern.

Back Stitched Chain Stitch

- Lay a row of chain stitch as a foundation.
- Bring the needle up through A and down through B in the middle of the chain stitches.
- Bring the needle up through C and down through A in the middle of the chain stitches.
- Continue this pattern, laying a row of back stitch directly over the top of the row of chain stitch.

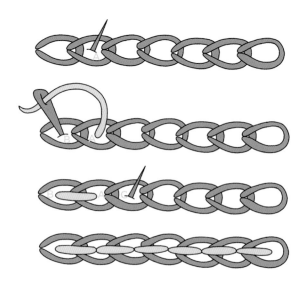

Lazy Daisy

- Bring the needle up through A.
- Pull the needle down through A, stopping when you have a small loop left behind on the front side of the fabric.
- Bring the needle up through B, pulling the thread through and keeping the petal flat and loose.
- Pull the needle down through C, tacking down the top of the petal.
- Bring the needle back up through or right next to A as the base of the next petal.

Fly Stitch

- Bring the needle up through A and down through B without pulling the thread taut against the fabric.
- Bring the needle up through C, which sits in the middle of A-B, and slightly below and down through D, tacking down the bottom of the stitch.

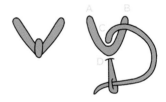

Seed Stitch

- Bring the needle up at A and down at B, just like a small straight stitch.
- Repeat these tiny stitches in random directions until you have filled the desired area.

Couching Stitch

- Bring one length of thread (foundation thread) up at A, leaving it loose on the front of the fabric.
- With a second length of thread (fastening thread), bring the needle up at B and down at C, tacking down the foundation thread.
- Continue the previous step at various intervals along the foundation thread, following the contour of the pattern lines.
- Once you have stitched enough fastening stitches, rethread the foundation thread onto the needle and tack it down at D.

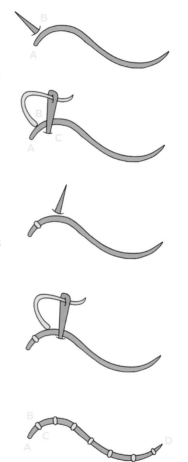

Long and Short Stitch

- Bring the needle up through A and down through B.
- Bring the needle up through C and down through D, alternating the length of each stitch in the first row.
- Once you start on the second row, maintain the length of the longer stitch, adding it below every stitch from the previous row.

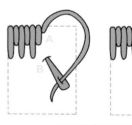

French Knot

- With your thread secured at the back of your fabric, pinch the thread approx. 5cm/2in above where it comes through the fabric and hold it taut.
- Place your needle in front of the thread between your non-needle hand and the fabric.
- Wind thread around the needle twice while continuing to hold the thread taut.
- Insert the tip of the needle into the fabric near the same hole where your thread emerges from the fabric.
- Again, pull the thread taut with your non-needle hand so that the tightly-wound thread slides down the needle and sits against the fabric.
- Holding the thread taut in your non-needle hand, pull the needle through to the back of the fabric.

CHAPTER 1

Colorful Shapes

Project 1 **Geometric Heart**   28

Project 2 **Confetti**   34

Project 3 **Abstract Hoop**   38

Geometric Heart

This is a fantastic beginner project. I'm offering two (of many) options for how you can stitch this design. This project can be completed in less than an hour (a perfect last-minute yet thoughtful handmade gift!), or sit a little longer and enjoy stitching a more intricate piece over an evening or two.

 WHAT YOU'LL NEED:

- Geometric Heart Pattern (page 111)
- Your chosen fabric, approx. 10" x 10"
- Size 7 embroidery needle
- 6" embroidery hoop
- Small, sharp scissors
- Embroidery thread (see color suggestions within each design option)

STITCHES USED:

- Straight stitch
- Satin stitch

Option 1

Thread/Color suggestion:
Kreinik Very Fine #4 Braid in 021 - Copper

Step 1:
Using two strands of thread, use a straight stitch to trace the outline of each geometric shape that makes up the heart.

> **NOTE:** *This is a metallic thread. I often keep well clear of metallic threads as they are notoriously tricky to work with, however, the end result is worth the try, in my opinion! Of course, you can use whatever color thread (and fabric) you desire, giving you endless options.*

Option 2

Thread/Color suggestion:
DMC 6 stranded embroidery thread in the following colors: 452, 518, 729, 993, 3799

Step 1:
Using three strands of thread and a different color for each triangular element, use satin stitches to fill the triangles. Work each triangle in a different direction, starting from the middle of the base up to the point. Refer to the diagram for the stitching direction of each triangle.

Step 2 (optional):
If you're not happy with your level of tidiness where your triangles meet, you could consider completing the embroidery with Option One and adding a row of straight stitches to outline each of the triangular elements in a contrasting color.

NOTE: *Since there is less surface area at the triangle points than at the bases, some of your satin stitches near the points may overlap.*

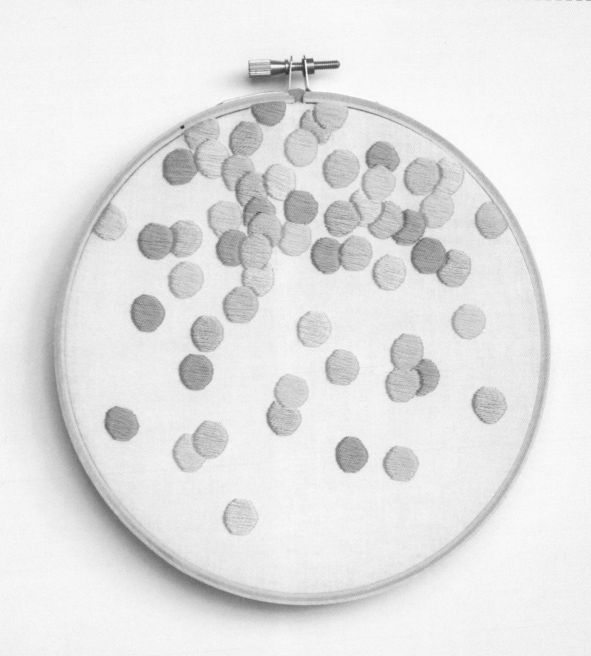

Confetti

- -

It's the kind of confetti that you wouldn't mind having spilled—over fabric, that is! This colorful design uses just one embroidery stitch; the satin stitch. You will master this stitch by the time you finish!

 WHAT YOU'LL NEED:

- Confetti pattern (page 113)
- Your chosen fabric, approx. 10" x 10"
- Size 7 embroidery needle
- 6" embroidery hoop
- Small, sharp scissors
- DMC embroidery thread in the following colors: 211, 472, 598, 603, 743, 993, 3824

STITCHES USED:

- Satin stitch

Use three strands of thread for the entire project.

Step 1:

Refer to the diagram to determine which color to use where; satin stitch each piece of confetti horizontally.

Abstract Hoop

What started as an experiment in abstract design resulted in a fun little stitch sampler made with four simple stitches! Each element is filled with one of the four embroidery stitches listed below, leaving you with a great example of how you can add loads of texture and variety within a single embroidery piece.

 WHAT YOU'LL NEED:

- Abstract Hoop pattern (page 115)
- Your chosen fabric, approx. 10" x 10"
- Size 7 embroidery needle
- 6" embroidery hoop
- Small, sharp scissors
- DMC embroidery thread in the following colors: 224, 225, 833, 924, 3024, 3817

STITCHES USED:

- Back stitch
- Satin stitch
- Chain stitch
- French knot

Use three strands of thread for the entire design. The numbered diagram on page 43 shows the best order to stitch the various elements that make up this design.

Step 1:
Fill with satin stitch using DMC 833.

Step 2:
Fill with French knots using DMC 225.

Step 3:
Fill with satin stitch using DMC 225.

Step 4:
Fill with chain stitch using DMC 224, working in a circular motion from the outer border in.

Step 5:
Fill with back stitch using DMC 833, offset between the rows in a brick-like pattern.

Step 6:
Fill with satin stitch using DMC 225.

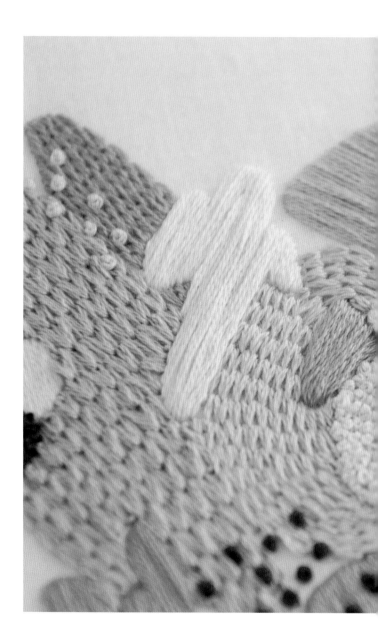

Step 7:
Fill with French knots using DMC 924.

Step 8:
Fill with satin stitch using DMC 833.

Step 9:
Fill with chain stitch using DMC 3817, working in rows starting at the top and alternating the direction with each row.

Step 10:
Fill with satin stitch using DMC 224.

Step 11:
Fill with chain stitch using DMC 3024, working in a circular motion from the outer border in.

Step 12:
Fill with back stitch using DMC 924, offset between the rows in a brick-like pattern.

Step 13:
Fill with satin stitch using DMC 833.

Step 14:
Fill with satin stitch using DMC 224.

Step 15:
Fill with back stitch using DMC 3024, offset between the rows in a brick-like pattern.

Step 16:
Fill with French knots using DMC 3817.

Step 17:
Fill with satin stitch using 3817.

Step 18:
Fill with chain stitch using DMC 924, working in rows starting at the top and alternating the direction with each row.

Step 19:
Stitch a scattering of French knots using DMC 3024 (a), 224 (b), 924 (c), 225 (d).

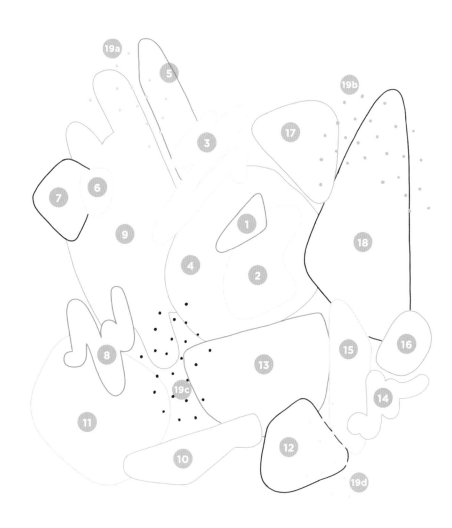

plant
lif

CHAPTER 2

Florals

Project 4 **Floral Curtain**   **46**

Project 5 **Leafy Wreath**   **50**

Project 6 **Gardener Girl**   **54**

Project 7 **Vase of Flowers**   **58**

Floral Curtain

I've always adored those beautiful floral backdrops that cascade down behind the happy couple at weddings. This pattern is an oh-so-pretty, pint-sized version that uses just three embroidery stitches!

 WHAT YOU'LL NEED:

- Floral Curtain Pattern (page 117)
- Your chosen fabric, approx. 10" x 10"
- Size 8 embroidery needle
- 6" embroidery hoop
- Small, sharp scissors
- DMC embroidery thread in the following colors: 168, 224, 505, 722, 3808, 3820

STITCHES USED:

- Back stitch
- Satin stitch
- French knot

Use two strands of thread for the entire design.

Step 1:
Vines:
Back stitch from the top down, stopping to fill each leaf in with satin stitch using DMC 505.

Step 2:
Starting on the far left vine, stitch the flowers from the top down:
A. Satin stitch using DMC 722. Stitch the smaller petal at a slightly different angle to define the petals.
B. Cluster of French knots using DMC 3820.
C. Satin stitch using DMC 224.
D. Satin stitch using DMC 3808.

Step 3:
A. Satin stitch using DMC 3820.
B. Satin stitch using DMC 3808.
C. Cluster of French knots using DMC 168.
D. Satin stitch using DMC 3820.
E. Cluster of French knots using DMC 224.

Step 4:
A. Satin stitch using DMC 224.
B. Cluster of French knots using DMC 722.
C. Satin stitch using DMC 168.
D. Satin stitch using DMC 3808.
E. Cluster of French knots using DMC 168.
F. Satin stitch using DMC 224.

Step 5:
A. Satin stitch using DMC 3820.
B. Cluster of French knots using DMC 224.
C. Satin stitch using DMC 722.
D. Satin stitch using DMC 3808.

Step 6:
A. Cluster of French knots using DMC 3808.
B. Satin stitch using DMC 224.
C. Cluster of French knots using DMC 168.
D. Satin stitch using DMC 3808.
E. Satin stitch using DMC 224.
F. Cluster of French knots using DMC 722.
G. Satin stitch using DMC 3820.

Step 7:

A. Satin stitch using DMC 168.
B. Cluster of French knots using DMC 3820.
C. Satin stitch using DMC 3808.
D. Satin stitch using DMC 224.

Step 8:

A. Cluster of French knots using DMC 722.
B. Satin stitch using DMC 168.
C. Satin stitch using DMC 224.
D. Cluster of French knots using DMC 3808.
E. Satin stitch using DMC 3820.

NOTE:
When you are preparing to finish and frame the embroidery in the hoop, position the fabric so that the tops of the vines will be folded between the inner and outer hoops, creating an effect of the vines cascading over.

Leafy Wreath

If you're a self-confessed plant lady (or man), you'll no doubt welcome an extra bit of greenery—of the stitched variety (especially if you struggle to keep real plants alive, like me!). Keep the leafy phrase in the middle of the wreath or change it up—it's entirely up to you.

 WHAT YOU'LL NEED:

- Leafy Wreath Pattern (page 119)
- Your chosen fabric, approx. 12" x 12"
- Size 8 embroidery needle
- 8" embroidery hoop
- Small, sharp scissors
- DMC embroidery thread in the following colors: 310, 420, 502, 503, 644, 924, 3362

STITCHES USED:

- Back stitch
- Satin stitch
- Fishbone stitch
- French knot

Step 1:

Fill in the large leaves with satin stitch using DMC 503. Start at the top center of the leaf and work your way down the sides, angling your stitches and overlapping them when needed to emphasize the organic shape of the leaves. Using the same color, stitch the stems with back stitch.

Step 2:

Stitch along the branches of the medium-sized leaves with back stitch using DMC 502, stopping at each leaf to fill it in. Stitch the larger leaves with fishbone stitch and the smaller leaves with satin stitch.

Step 3:

Stitch along the branches of the small-sized leaves with back stitch using DMC 3362, stopping at each leaf to fill it in. Stitch the leaves with satin stitch.

Step 4:

Stitch along the branches of the silver leaves with back stitch using DMC 644, stopping at each leaf to fill it in. Stitch the leaves with satin stitch.

Step 5:

Stitch along the brown branches with back stitch using DMC 420.

Step 6:

Fill in the berries at the ends of the brown branches with satin stitch using DMC 924.

Step 7:

Use back stitch to stitch the text and a single French knot to dot the "i" using DMC 310.

plant
life

Gardener Girl

A flower as big as your head? Yes, please! This pretty lady with her huge protea is a quick project to stitch up. The flower is deceptively simple and makes a statement on darker fabric.

 WHAT YOU'LL NEED:

- Gardener Girl Pattern (page 121)
- Your chosen fabric, approx. 10" x 12"
- Size 8 embroidery needle
- 5" x 9" oval embroidery hoop
- Small, sharp scissors
- DMC embroidery thread in the following colors: 225, 310, 367, 420, 761, 988, ECRU

STITCHES USED:

- Back stitch
- Whipped back stitch
- Straight stitch
- Satin stitch
- French knot

Use two strands of thread for the flower (unless otherwise specified in the steps below) and one strand of thread for the girl.

Step 1:
Outline the flower petals with whipped back stitch using DMC 225. Use a single strand of thread for the foundational back stitch layer and two strands of thread for the whipped layer.

Step 2:
Outline the leaves with whipped back stitch using DMC 988. Use a single strand of thread for the foundational back stitch layer and two strands of thread for the whipped layer.

Step 3:
Fill in the flower petals with satin stitch using DMC 225 for the petals at the front and DMC 761 for the petals at the back.

Step 4:
Fill in most of the leaves with satin stitch using DMC 988.

Step 5:

Fill in the other leaves with satin stitch using DMC 367. Refer to the diagram and close-up images to determine the color to stitch each of the leaves.

Step 6:

Fill in the center of the flower with straight stitches in a variety of lengths using DMC ECRU. Use longer stitches around the outside of the center and gradually make your stitches smaller as you work toward the middle. Randomly place some straight stitches in DMC 225 throughout the center.

Step 7:

Fill in the stem of the flower with horizontal satin stitch using DMC 420.

Step 8:

Using a single strand of thread, back stitch the entire outline of the girl using DMC 310.

Vase of Flowers

I've grouped together some of my favorite flowers to create this pattern. Peonies, anemones, dahlias—who wouldn't want a huge bunch of these to hold onto?! This pattern is more detailed than the ones before it, however it uses simple embroidery stitches and the end result is worth the effort!

 WHAT YOU'LL NEED:

- Vase of Flowers Pattern (page 123)
- Your chosen fabric, approx. 10" x 10"
- Size 8 embroidery needle
- 6" embroidery hoop
- Small, sharp scissors
- DMC embroidery thread in the following colors: 224, 225, 310, 316, 420, 648, 924, 3052, 3362, 3803, 3811, 3820, ECRU

STITCHES USED:

- Back stitch
- Whipped back stitch
- Satin stitch
- Fishbone stitch
- French knot
- Fly stitch
- Seed stitch
- Straight stitch

Use two strands of thread
for the entire design, unless
otherwise specified.

Step 1:
Pink peonies:

Outline the petals with whipped back stitch using DMC 224.

Step 2:
Pink peonies:

Fill in the petals with satin stitch using DMC 225.

Step 3:
Peony on the left:

Fill in the center of the flower with seed stitch using DMC 3820.

Step 4:
Anemone:

Outline the petals with whipped back stitch using DMC ECRU.

Step 5:
Anemone:

Fill in the petals with satin stitch using DMC ECRU.

Step 6:
Anemone:

Fill in the center of the flower with seed stitch using DMC 924. Using one strand of thread, randomly place little straight stitches from around the center of the flower outward. Top them with a French knot using DMC 924.

Step 7:
Dahlia:

Outline the petals with fly stitch using DMC 3803.

Step 8:
Dahlia:

Fill in the petals with satin stitch using DMC 316.

Step 9:
Larger leaves:

Fill each leaf with fishbone stitch using DMC 3052.

Step 10:
Smaller leaves:

Back stitch along the branches, stopping at each leaf and filling it with satin stitch using DMC 3362.

Step 11:
Tiny blue flower buds:

Back stitch along the branches using DMC 3362.

Step 12:
Tiny blue flower buds:
Randomly stitch a cluster of French knots around each of the branches using DMC 3811.

Step 13:
Small dark mauve flowers:
Fill in the petals with satin stitch in DMC 3803.

Step 14:
Branches:
Back stitch along these using DMC 420.

Step 15:
Berries:
Fill these in with satin stitch using DMC 924.

Step 16:
Vase:
Fill in the pot with satin stitch using DMC 648.

Step 17:
Hands:
Back stitch along the outline of the hands, stopping to fill in the fingernails with satin stitch, using DMC 310.

Step 18:
Tiny flower bud clusters:
Using DMC ECRU, randomly stitch clusters of French knots around some of the flowers and leaves. Use these to fill in little empty spaces and to add some extra buds where you want them.

CHAPTER 3
Collaborations

- -

Project 8 **Gardens Heart by Lauren Merrick**   66

Project 9 **Flowers and Thread by Alli Koch**   72

Project 10 **Enjoy Today by Audrey Smit**   76

Gardens Heart

Gardens Heart is a collaborative pattern with Australian illustrator Lauren Merrick. Lauren creates beautiful illustrations with watercolor, gouache, paper cut, collage, and ink. Her art is often influenced by the Australian flora and fauna that surround her in the beautiful Blue Mountains of New South Wales. Lauren and I are repeat collaborators and her whimsical designs translate so well to embroidery!

 WHAT YOU'LL NEED:

- Gardens Heart pattern (page 125)
- Your chosen fabric, approx. 12" x 12"
- Size 8 embroidery needle
- 8" embroidery hoop
- Small, sharp scissors
- DMC embroidery thread in the following colors: 310, 351, 523, 796, 924, 3829, BLANC

STITCHES USED:

- Back stitch
- Straight stitch
- Satin stitch
- French knot
- Long and short stitch

Step 1:

Fill in the center of the whole flowers and tops of the half flowers with satin stitch using DMC 3829. With the same color, stitch small straight stitches around the centers of the whole flowers.

Step 2:

Fill in the base of the petals with satin stitch using DMC 351. As the flowers are small, it will only require two or three stitches to fill in these elements.

Step 3:

Fill in the tops of the petals with satin stitch using DMC 3829. As above, it will only require two or three stitches to fill these.

Step 4:

Fill in the large leaves with fishbone stitch using DMC 924.

Step 5:

Using DMC 924, stitch along the branches of the leafy segments, including the small branches of the woman's "heart" at the center of the piece and the stems of the strawberries.

Step 6:

Fill in the long skinny leaves with satin stitch using DMC 523.

Step 7:

Using one strand of thread in DMC 523, stitch French knots around the women's "heart" branches at the center of the pattern.

Step 8:

Fill in the small, round leaves with satin stitch using DMC 523. A few of the leaves are two-toned, using half DMC 523 and half DMC 924. Refer to the diagram to determine which of these leaves are two-toned.

Step 9:

Working over the top of the satin stitch on the small round leaves, stitch straight stitches on some of the leaves. Refer to the diagram to determine where to place these stitches.

Step 10:
Fill in the birds bodies with satin stitch using the following colors: DMC 796, 3829, 351 and BLANC (for the small patch on the birds back). Fill in the beaks with satin stitch using DMC 310 and stitch a single French knot using the same color for the eyes.

Step 11:
Fill in the tops of the strawberries with satin stitch using DMC 523.

Step 12:
Working vertically from the top down, fill in the strawberries with long and short stitch using DMC 351. Stitch "seeds" with tiny straight stitches over the top using one strand of DMC 310.

Step 13:
With one strand of thread in DMC 310, stitch the woman's outline and facial features. Back stitch the eyes and mouth using a couple of very tiny stitches. With one strand of thread in DMC 351, satin stitch the woman's cheek with small stitches.

Flowers and Thread

Flowers and Thread is a collaborative pattern with illustrator Alli Koch. Alli is well-known for her beautiful, monochromatic floral illustrations and fabulous wall murals she has done all over the United States. Her delicate floral designs translated into needle and thread are a match made in heaven!

 WHAT YOU'LL NEED:

- Flowers and Thread pattern (page 127)
- Your chosen fabric, approx. 12" x 12"
- Size 5 & 8 embroidery needles
- 8" embroidery hoop
- Small, sharp scissors
- DMC embroidery thread in the following color: 310

STITCHES USED:

- Back stitch
- Lazy Daisy
- French knot
- Satin stitch
- Couching stitch

Use two strands of thread for this design unless otherwise specified.

Step 1:
Stitch your way around the hand with back stitch, stopping at the fingers to fill in the finger nails with satin stitch.

Step 2:
Fill the centers of the large flowers with satin stitch.

Step 3:
Work around the outlines of the flowers and leaves with back stitch.

Step 4:
Stitch along the branches of smaller leaves with back stitch, stopping at each leaf to stitch them with lazy daisy.

Step 5:
Using one strand of thread, fill in all the lines of definition on the flowers with back stitch.

Step 6:
Using one strand, randomly place a few French knots around the centers of the larger, open flowers.

Step 7:
Stitch along the needle using back stitch.

Step 8:
Create the strand of thread with couching stitch. Use all six strands of thread and the size 5 needle for the foundation and one strand of thread and the size 8 needle for the fastening stitches. It's up to you how long you leave this strand of thread that the hand is holding!

Enjoy Today

Enjoy Today is a collaborative pattern with children's clothing designer and illustrator Audrey Smit. Audrey's charming designs feature vibrant floral arrangements and patterns that burst with color and life. They are so joyful to look at and translate beautifully into embroidered works of art!

 WHAT YOU'LL NEED:

- Enjoy Today pattern (page 129)
- Your chosen fabric, approx. 12" x 12"
- Size 5 & 8 embroidery needles
- 8" embroidery hoop
- Small, sharp scissors
- DMC embroidery thread in the following colors: 26, 28, 32, 225, 316, 372, 520, 962, 3727, 3820, 3828, 3832

STITCHES USED:

- Back stitch
- Straight stitch
- Satin stitch
- Couching stitch
- French knot
- Split stitch

Use two strands of thread for this design unless otherwise specified. The numbered diagram on the following pages shows the best order to stitch the various elements in the design.

Step 1:
Fill in the main part of the large purple flowers with satin stitch using DMC 26.

Step 2:
Fill in the smaller part at the top of the purple flowers with satin stitch using DMC 28.

Step 3:
Using DMC 32 and one strand of thread, stitch a few random straight stitches topped with a French knot to create the stamen of the flower.

Step 4:
Fill in the main part of the large and medium pink flowers with satin stitch using DMC 962.

Step 5:
Fill in the center of the pink flowers with satin stitch using DMC 3832.

Step 6:
Fill in the top part of the pink flowers with satin stitch using DMC 225.

Step 7:
Fill in the bases of the small mauve flowers with satin stitch using DMC 316.

Step 8:
Fill in the tops of the small mauve flowers with satin stitch using DMC 3727.

Step 9:
Fill in the center of the yellow flowers with satin stitch using DMC 3822.

Step 10:
Fill in the yellow flowers with satin stitch using DMC 3820.

Step 11:
Fill in the leaves with fishbone stitch and the branches with back stitch using DMC 520.

Step 12:
Fill in the small leaves that are paired with the yellow flowers with satin stitch using DMC 372.

Step 13:
Stitch a line along the centers of the leaves with split stitch using DMC 372.

Step 14:
Stitch the text with couching stitch using DMC 3828. Use all six strands of thread and the size 5 needle for the foundation and one strand of thread and the size 8 needle for the fastening stitches.

Step 15:
Using four strands of thread, stitch one French knot for the dot above the "j" using DMC 3828.

CHAPTER 4

Hoop-less Creations

Project 11 **Embroidered Patches**   84

Project 12 **Canvas Shoes**   92

Project 13 **Embroidered Clothing**   96

Project 14 **Candy Heart Tote**   102

Project 15 **Cushion**   106

Embroidered Patches

- -

Embroidered patches are a fun way to add a bit of personality to your clothing or accessories. They are quick to create and a great project to try when you want to venture away from the hoop.

 WHAT YOU'LL NEED:

- Embroidered Patches pattern (page 131)
- Heavier weight calico, approx. 8" x 8"
- Fusible interfacing
- HeatnBond® iron-on adhesive
- 4" embroidery hoop
- Small, sharp scissors
- DMC embroidery thread in the following colors:
  > Diamond - 25, 648, 931, 3341, 3689 (optional: Kreinik Metallics Very Fine #4 Braid in 001)
  > Strawberry - 310, 891, 3347
  > Avocado - 165, 780, 895, 3347
  > Peach - 20, 988, 3341, ECRU
  > Rainbow - 153, 165, 964, 3341, 3706, 3820, ECRU

STITCHES USED:

- Long and short stitch
- Chain stitch
- Back stitch
- Straight stitch
- Fishbone stitch
- Satin stitch

PREPARING THE FABRIC:

It is necessary to adhere a layer of interfacing on the back side of the fabric when stitching to increase durability and stop the fabric from fraying as you edge the patches. This is done prior to transferring the pattern onto fabric.

Step 1:

Lay your fabric on an ironing board; place the interfacing fusible-side down on top of the fabric. The fusible side will have a slight bumpiness to it and the adhesive will look a bit reflective if you hold it up to the light.

Step 2:

Lay a damp pressing cloth (eg. a clean tea towel) on top of the interfacing. Press down the iron for 15 seconds. If you need to move the iron to apply heat to another portion of the fabric, pick up the iron and set it down rather than gliding it.

Step 3:

Once the interfacing adheres to the fabric and the fabric is dry, you can proceed with transferring the pattern onto the fabric and fastening it into the embroidery hoop.

Use three strands of thread to stitch the patches.

DIAMOND:

Step 1:

Using the diagram to determine which color goes in which triangle, fill the triangles with long and short stitch, starting from the bottom of the triangle and stitching toward the tip.

Step 2:

Outline the triangles with back stitch using DMC 648 or Kreinik Metallics Very Fine #4 Braid in 001 (if you want to add a bit of sparkle).

Edging color: DMC 648

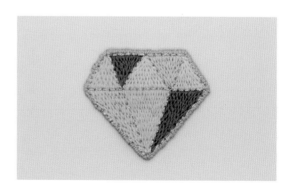

STRAWBERRY:

Step 1:

Fill the top of the strawberry with long and short stitch, starting in the center and working out toward the tips of each of the leaves using DMC 3347. It's okay to overlap some of the stitches in the center so that there is no obvious "starting point".

Step 2:

Fill in the strawberry with long and short stitch using DMC 891. Start from the top down, reducing the number of stitches in the rows as you get closer to the bottom. If you realize that you have some empty spots, just go back and fill them in with a straight stitch or two.

Step 3:

Create the "seeds" with randomly placed straight stitches using DMC 310.

Edging color: DMC 310

NOTE:
When using long and short stitch and working along the curve or direction of the shape you are filling, you may need to reduce the number of stitches in some rows as you get closer to the smaller end of the shape. You might be left with some empty spots; you can go back and fill these in with a straight stitch or two.

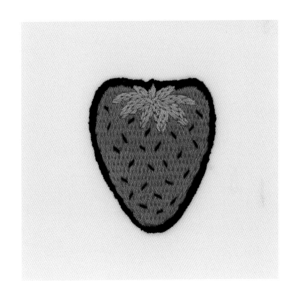

AVOCADO:

Step 1:

Fill in the seed with chain stitch using DMC 780. Stitch in a circular pattern from the outside in, starting a new row each time you have finished a round.

Step 2:

Fill in the middle section of the avocado with chain stitch using DMC 165. Stitch in a circular pattern from the outside in, starting a new row each time you have finished a round. Fill in the portion directly above the top of the seed with some shorter rows of chain stitch, following the same direction as the rows you have already stitched.

Step 3:

Fill in the outer section of the avocado with chain stitch using DMC 3347. Stitch in a circular pattern from the outside in, starting a new row each time you have finished a round.

Edging color: DMC 895

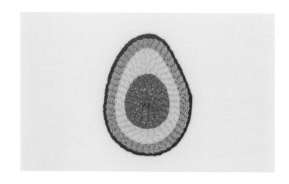

NOTE:
When using chain stitch to fill your patches, try to pull the stitches tight and stitch the rows very close together so that there is very little fabric showing through the stitches.

PEACH:

Step 1:

Using the diagram to determine where the starting point is, fill in the peach with chain stitch using DMC 3341. Once you have filled in the smaller (right) side of the peach up to the lighter section, keep going in a circular motion around the larger (left) side of the peach, stopping when you reach the lighter section on that side.

Step 2:

Using DMC 20, fill in the lighter sections with chain stitch, continuing in the same direction as the darker peach stitches.

Step 3:

Fill in the leaves with fishbone stitch using DMC 988.

Edging color: DMC ECRU

RAINBOW:

Step 1:

Using the diagram to determine which color goes with which stripe, fill the stripes with chain stitch, starting at one side and alternating the direction of the rows until you have filled the stripe. Some stripes may require an additional, shorter row of chain stitch in parts, as the rainbow stripes are intentionally a bit lopsided. The stripes will require fewer rows as you get closer to the middle of the rainbow.

Edging color: DMC ECRU

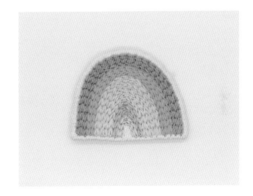

FINISHING THE PATCHES:

I am providing instructions for one method to secure your patches onto the item of clothing or accessory you are decorating: use an iron-on adhesive called HeatnBond. If you do not want to adhere your patches this way, you can instead simply sew them onto your item.

Step 1:

Using your marker, draw an outline around the patch approx. 2mm away from your stitching. This measurement is approximation; you can draw the outline farther away from your stitching if you prefer a thicker edge.

Step 2:

With sharp fabric scissors, cut around your outline.

Step 3:

Use satin stitch to create an edge around your patch. The edging colors have been noted in the individual instructions for each patch. Poke your needle from the back through to the front of the fabric and then repeat over and over so that you are completely covering your raw fabric edge in satin stitch.

Step 4:

Trace onto and cut out a piece of Heatnbond; this piece should be ever-so-slightly smaller than your patch.

Step 5:

With your iron on medium heat and without steam, place adhesive on the back side of the patch. The paper liner should face up.

Step 6:

Place and hold the iron for two seconds. Allow to cool and then peel off the paper liner.

Step 7:

Place your patch adhesive side down onto the item of clothing or accessory you are decorating. Press and hold the iron for eight seconds (using a cloth in between the iron and any metallic stitches).

Step 8:

If you are working with a thicker material like denim, iron for an additional two seconds from the inside of the denim.

Refer to the instructions on the HeatnBond packet for further information.

Canvas Shoes

- -

This is a really fun way to turn a simple pair of canvas shoes into a vibrant piece of wearable art! There are three size options for this pattern so that you can choose the size that best fits your shoes.

 WHAT YOU'LL NEED:
- Canvas Shoe Pattern (page 133)
- Plain canvas shoes
- Size 5 embroidery needle
- Small, sharp scissors
- DMC embroidery thread in the following colors: 369, 3362, 3706

STITCHES USED:
- Back stitch
- Satin stitch

Use three strands of thread for the design.

Step 1:

Refer to the diagram to determine which color goes where; fill the elements with satin stitch.

Step 2:

Working from the point where you finished the pink satin stitching of the stem toward the tip of the leaf, stitch a line of back stitch using DMC 3706.

> **NOTE:**
> *A simple way to transfer the design onto the shoes is by using a product called Sticky Fabri-Solvy by Sulky. Print directly onto it, cut around the design, then stick it directly to the shoe. Once you've finished stitching, it easily dissolves as you soak it in a bit of water. Refer to the package for detailed instructions.*

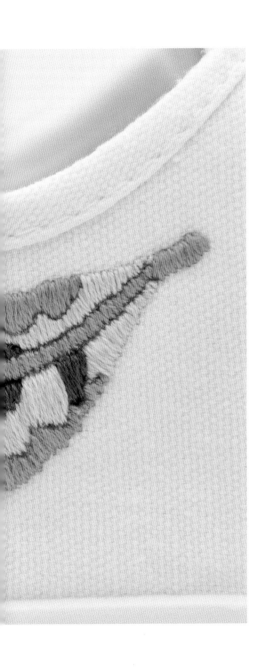

Embroidered Clothing

Give new life to a piece of clothing by stitching a sweet design! Use any or all of the designs and basic instructions I've provided to stitch on whatever clothing item you like, wherever you like! There is no wrong place to put these little designs. The possibilities are endless!

 WHAT YOU'LL NEED:

- Embroidered Clothing pattern (page 135)
- Clothing item of choice
- Fusible interfacing (optional)
- Size 5 embroidery needle
- 4" embroidery hoop
- Small, sharp scissors
- DMC embroidery thread in the following colors: 04, 931, ECRU

STITCHES USED:

- Back stitch
- Satin stitch
- French knot

DAISIES:

Stitch a few on a pocket or randomly scatter them across your shirt (see pictured example).

Use all six strands of thread for the daisies. Color suggestions: DMC 931 (centers), DMC ECRU (petals)

Step 1:
Fill the center of the daisy with satin stitch.

Step 2:
Satin stitch eight evenly spaced petals each with three stitches.

> **NOTE:**
> *Depending on the thickness and color of the fabric of your item of clothing, you may need to consider other transfer options than the traditional tracing method. A light-colored carbon tracing paper works well on darker fabrics and Sulky Fabri-Solvi is a good choice for heavier fabrics like denim.*

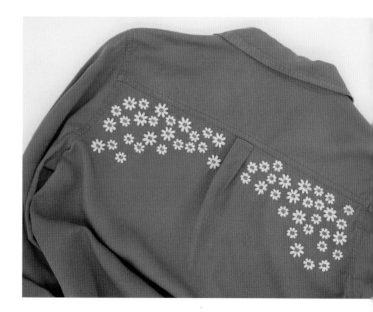

LITTLE POSY OF FLOWERS:

Use three strands of thread for this design.

Color suggestion: DMC 04

Step 1:
Stitch the flowers with satin stitch in a horizontal direction, as it is important to keep the stitches short.

Step 2:
Stitch along the stems with back stitch, stopping at the leaves and tiny flower buds to fill them with satin stitch as you go.

LEAFY BRANCHES:

The pattern template for this design includes both directions, making them perfect for shirt collars or sleeve cuffs.

Use three strands of thread for this design. Color suggestion: DMC 931

Step 1:
Stitch along the stems with back stitch, stopping at the leaves to fill them with satin stitch as you go.

BONJOUR:

Use all six strands for this design.

Color suggestion: ECRU

Step 1:

Stitch along the letters with back stitch, adding a French knot above the "j."

To ensure your stitches are secured on the inside of your clothing item, line them with a layer of fusible interfacing, which will give them a bit of protection.

Step 1:

Cut a piece of interfacing just large enough to cover the stitched area.

Step 2:

Lay your item of clothing on top of a clean soft towel (this helps to not flatten your stitching) on your ironing board with the back side of the stitches facing up. Lay the fusible interfacing down over the top of the stitches. The fusible side will have a slight bumpiness to it and the adhesive will look a bit reflective if you hold it up to the light.

Step 3:

Lay a damp pressing cloth (e.g., a clean tea towel) on top of the interfacing. Press the iron down for fifteen seconds. If you need to move the iron to apply heat to another portion of the fabric, pick up the iron and set it down rather than gliding it.

Candy Heart Tote

We can all use the reminder to "Love More". Stitch this message on a tote to share with anyone around you!

 WHAT YOU'LL NEED:

- Candy Heart pattern (page 137)
- Cotton or light canvas tote bag
- Fusible interfacing (optional)
- Size 5 embroidery needle
- 8" or 10" embroidery hoop
- Small, sharp scissors
- DMC embroidery thread in the following colors: 3706, 3761, 3766

STITCHES USED:

- Back stitch
- Long and Short stitch
- Back stitched chain stitch

Step 1:

Fill in the text using long and short stitch in the thicker sections of the letters and back stitch along the thinner parts with DMC 3760.

Step 2:

Outline the top and lower inner edge of the heart using chain stitch with DMC 3761.

Step 3:

Outline the bottom edge of the heart using chain stitch with DMC 3766.

Step 4:

Stitch a row of back stitch into the middle of the chain stitch along the top, curved edge of the heart with DMC 3761. Work from where the lines meet on one side over to the same point on the other side.

Step 5:

Following from where you finished Step 4, stitch a row of back stitch into the middle of the chain stitch along the lower inner edge of the heart with DMC 3766.

Step 6:

Stitch a row of back stitch along the bottom edge of the heart into the middle of the chain stitch with DMC 3766.

Cushion

Customize a plain cushion cover with these easy little leafy motifs. Scatter them randomly or evenly space them in a pattern across the cushion cover—the choice is yours!

NOTE: Each motif also has a reverse pattern to give you variety as you arrange the elements on the cushion cover.

 WHAT YOU'LL NEED:
- Cushion patterns (page 139)
- 18" x 18" plain cushion cover
- Fusible interfacing (optional)
- Size 5 embroidery needle
- 4" embroidery hoop
- Small, sharp scissors
- DMC embroidery thread in the following colors: 3820

STITCHES USED:
- Back stitch
- Satin stitch
- Fishbone stitch

There are five leafy motifs for this project. Each of them has a reverse pattern as well. Use three strands of thread for the entire design.

Pattern #1:
Back stitch along the branch, stopping at each leaf to fill in with satin stitch.

Pattern #2:
Fill in the leaves with fishbone stitch, finishing each with a single straight stitch for the stem.

Pattern #3:
Back stitch along the branch and stems, stopping at each leaf to fill in with satin stitch.

Pattern #4:
Fill in the leaves with fishbone stitch. Stitch along the stems with back stitch. Fill in the flower buds with satin stitch.

Pattern #5:
Fill in the leaves with fishbone stitch. Stitch along the branches with back stitch.

To ensure your stitches are secured on the inside of your cushion, you can line the inside of the cushion with a layer of fusible interfacing, which will give them a bit of protection.

Step 1:
Cut a piece of interfacing large enough to cover the stitched area.

Step 2:
Lay your cushion inside out on top of a clean, soft towel (this helps to not flatten your stitching) on your ironing board with the back side of the stitches face up. Lay the fusible interfacing over the top of the stitches. The fusible side will have a slight bumpiness to it and the adhesive will look a bit reflective if you hold it up to the light.

Step 3:
Lay a damp pressing cloth (e.g., a clean tea towel) on top of the interfacing. Press down the iron down for fifteen seconds. If you need to move the iron to apply heat to another portion of the fabric, pick up the iron and set it down rather than gliding it.

Patterns

GEOMETRIC HEART *instructions found on page 28*

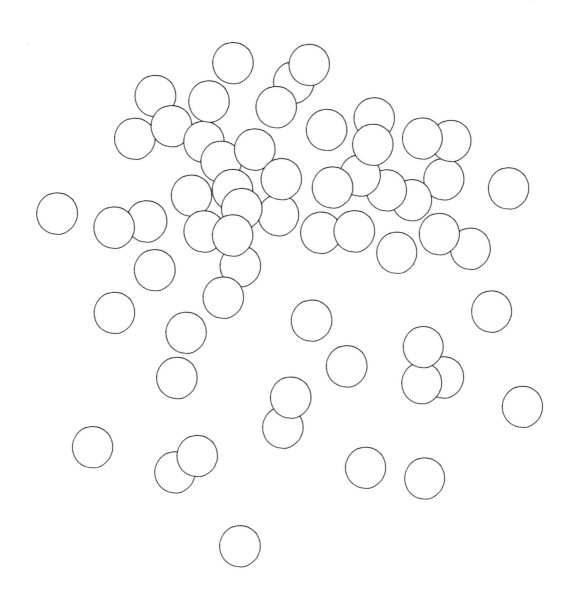

CONFETTI *instructions found on page 34*

ABSTRACT HOOP *instructions found on page 38*

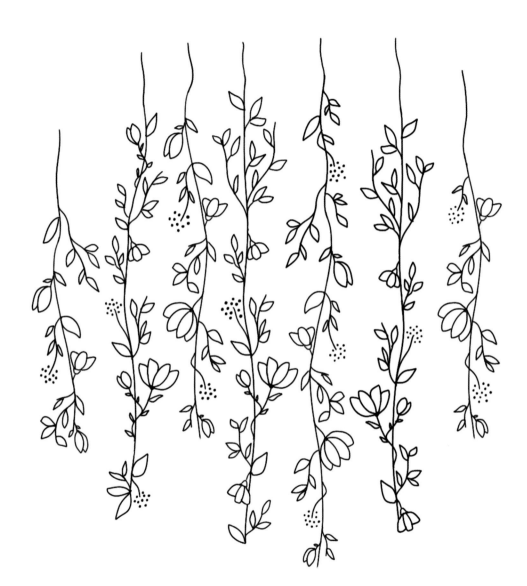

FLORAL CURTAIN *instructions found on page 46*

plant
life

LEAFY WREATH *instructions found on page 50*

GARDENER GIRL *instructions found on page 54*

VASE OF FLOWERS *instructions found on page 58*

GARDEN HEARTS by Lauren Merrick
instructions found on page 66

FLOWERS AND THREAD by Alli Koch
instructions found on page 72

ENJOY TODAY by Audrey Smit
instructions found on page 76

EMBROIDERED PATCHES *instructions found on page 84*

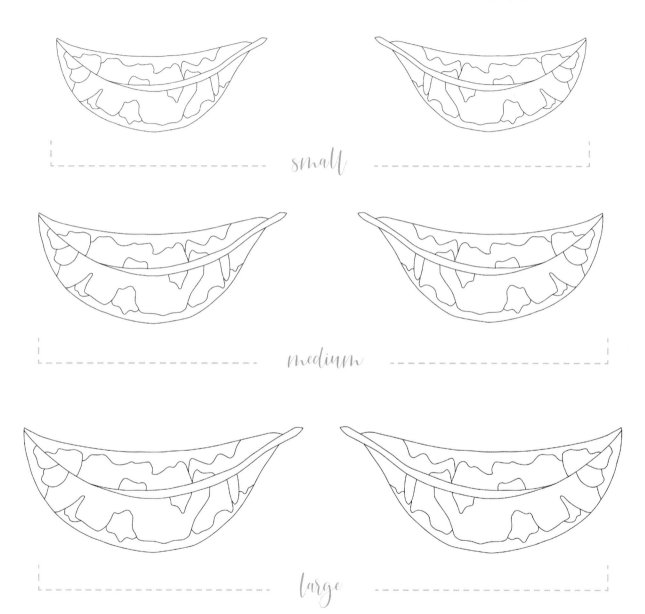

small

medium

large

CANVAS SHOES *instructions found on page 92*

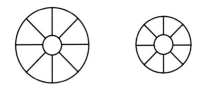

Bonjour

EMBROIDERED CLOTHING *instructions found on page 96*

CANDY HEART TOTE *instructions found on page 102*

CUSHION *instructions found on page 106*

Happy Stitching!

This project has been a dream come true and it is something that would not have come together without the help of some wonderful people.

I'd like to thank Clare, Chris, Alicia, and the team at Paige Tate & Co. Thank you for being so wonderful to work with. For all of your support, virtual hand-holding, flexibility, and encouragement!

Thank you to my lovely friends: photographer Bec Axon who has been so generous with her time and help with some of the beautiful photographs of my embroideries throughout the book; and florist Lillie Harris who created the delightful garland that borders the embroideries at the beginning of the "Florals" chapter.

I embarked on this project heavily pregnant with my fourth child and proceeded to work on it throughout the first six months of his life. I don't think I would have been willing to take the leap without the amazing support of my parents. Thank you, Mum and Dad, for all the babysitting, house cleaning, and meals that you offered so that I could spend time stitching and creating.

Finally, my boys—Logan, Hugo, Oliver and Remy. I love you and appreciate all of your hugs and kisses and compliments you often give to my embroideries! And to my husband, Derek, thank you for always being willing to act as a sounding board for my ideas and the way in which you challenge me creatively. You have given me endless encouragement, support, and help, and I am so incredibly grateful.

plant   life